D.I.Y. HAMSTERCRAFT

Mark Mowforth

David & Charles
Newton Abbot   London

Photoset & printed in Great Britain by
Redwood Burn Limited, Trowbridge, Wiltshire and
bound by Pegasus Bookbinding, Melksham, Wiltshire
for David & Charles Publishers plc
Brunel House   Newton Abbot   Devon

British Library Cataloguing in Publication Data

Mowforth, Mark
    D.I.Y. hamstercraft.
    I. Title
    828'.91409   PR6063.08/

    ISBN 0–7153–9134–8

To my inspiration, Hamid (R.I.P.)*, and his pet human, Anna.

With thanks to Mike De Luca, Bradley Dodd, my brother John and especially Sharon; — their help and support went way beyond the squeak of duty.

* I never touched him!.....

INTRODUCTION

For many years, inventive hamster-owners have been using their pets in ever more creative applications, with the result that some are no longer hamster-owners.

With the right degree of care however, a D.I.Y. enthusiast can slightly modify his hamster without significantly damaging it, and hence be rewarded with a Very Useful Thing.

It's easy to see why the hamster appeals to the imaginative do-it-yourselfer—it's small, furry, squashy and insoluble in water—and hence why a large number of successful 'hamstercraft' creations exist.

This book attempts, for the first time, to bring together a collection of such ideas. Most are illustrated with easy-to-follow instructions; those which I've not yet had the chance to carry out I have simply referred to, in case any experienced D.I.Y. enthusiasts wish to try them uninstructed.

It only remains for me to point out to any novice do-it-yourselfers that fortunately, many good hardware shops now stock hamster repair kits, and to wish you all many happy hamstercrafting hours.

D.I.Y. HAMSTERCRAFT
FOR
TOYMAKING/LEISURE

An ever popular area of hamstercrafting, but beware using Not Very Big hamsters in toys as toddlers have been known to pull these off and swallow them.

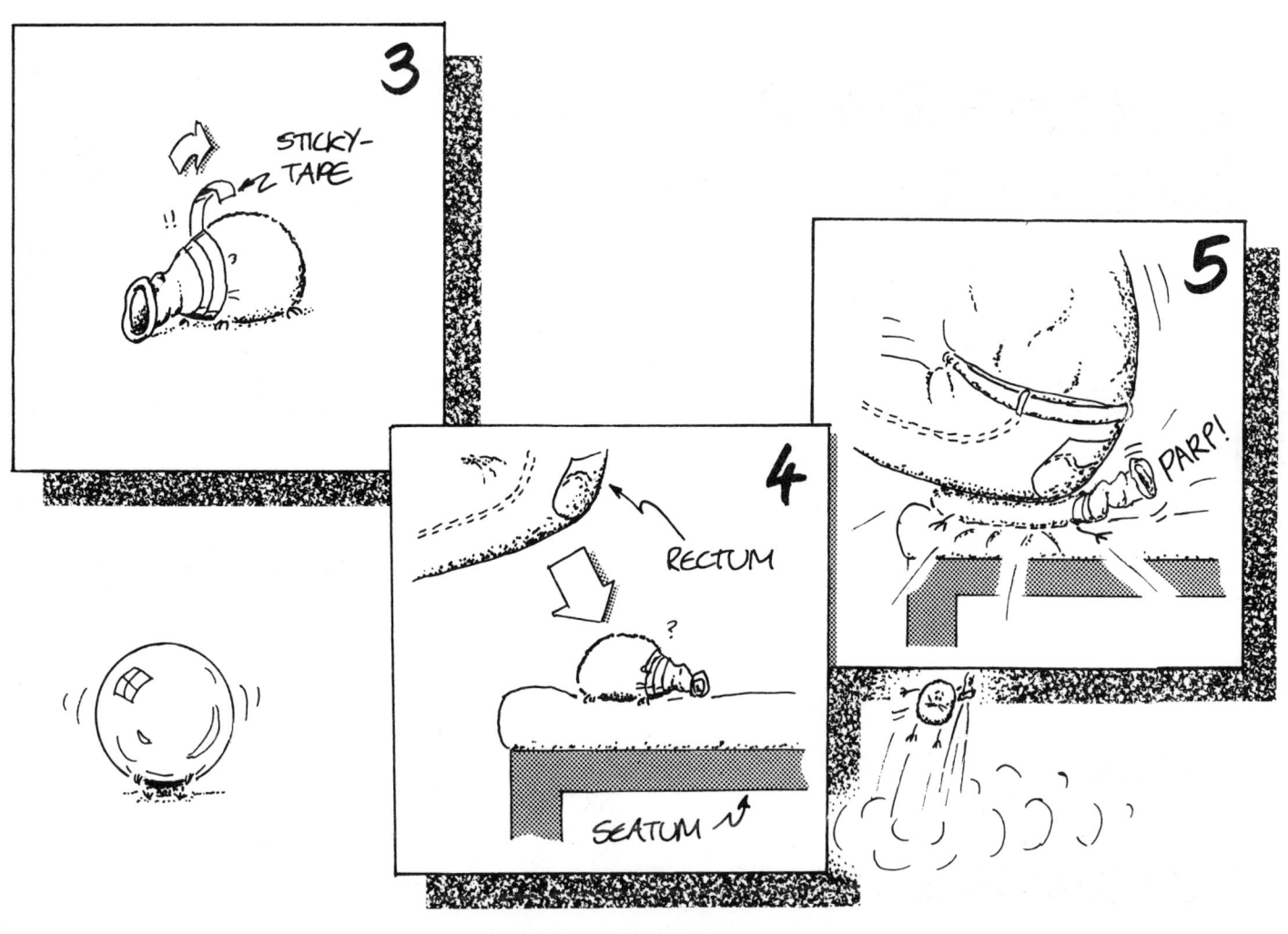

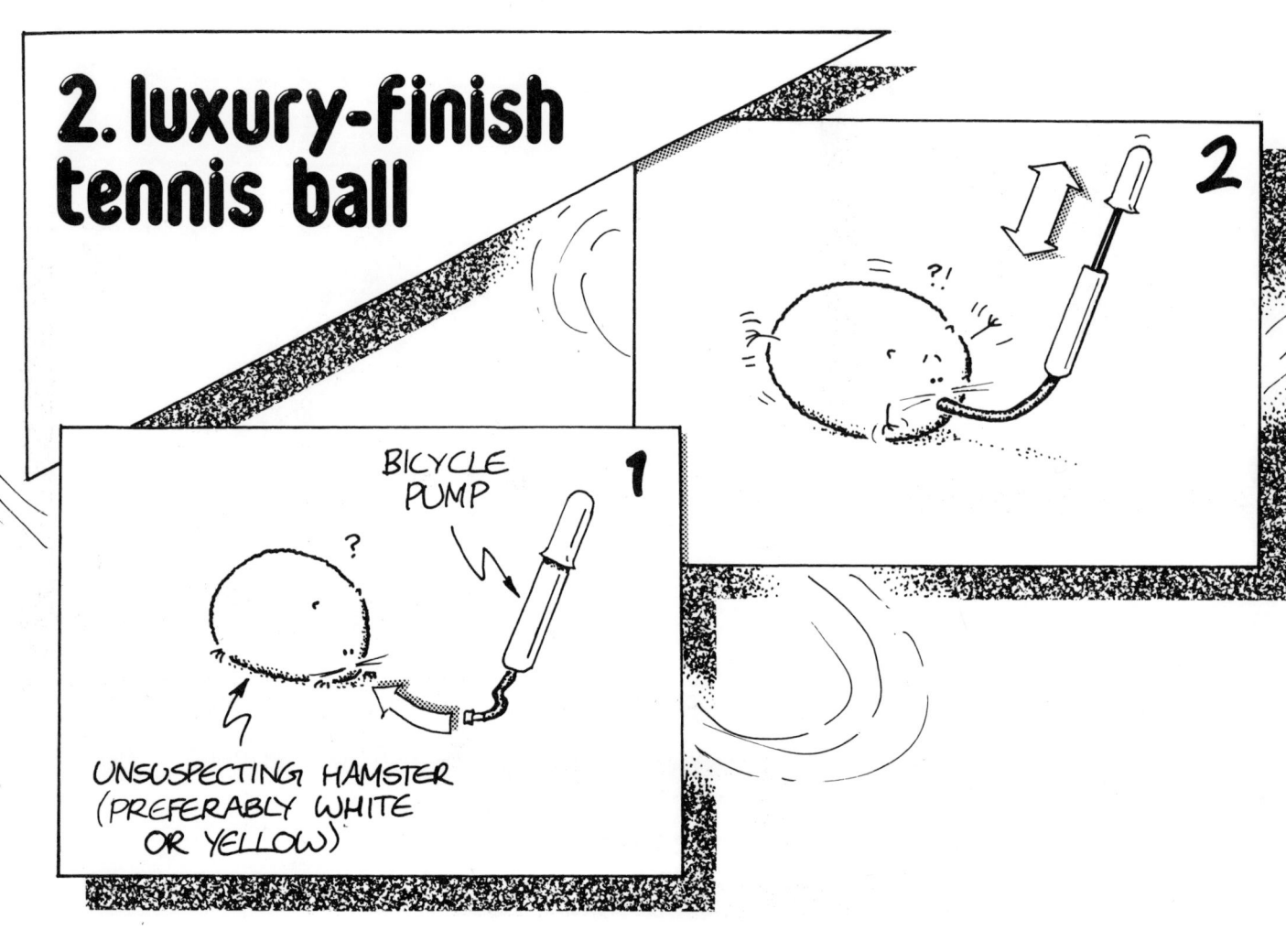

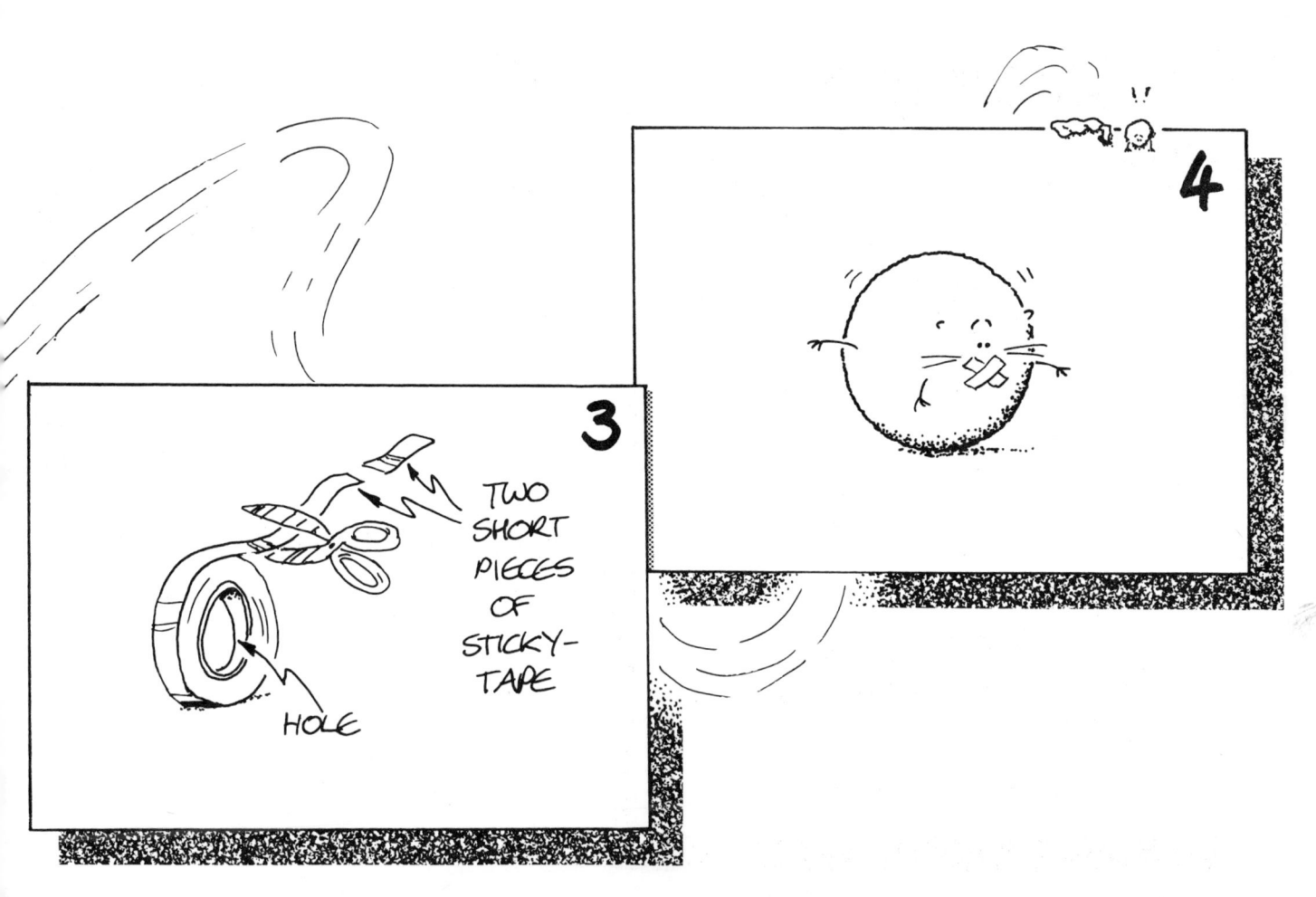

3

TWO SHORT PIECES OF STICKY-TAPE

HOLE

4

3. blackboard rubber

'FURRYFIX'® HAMSTER GLUE

2

BRUSH, IDIOT

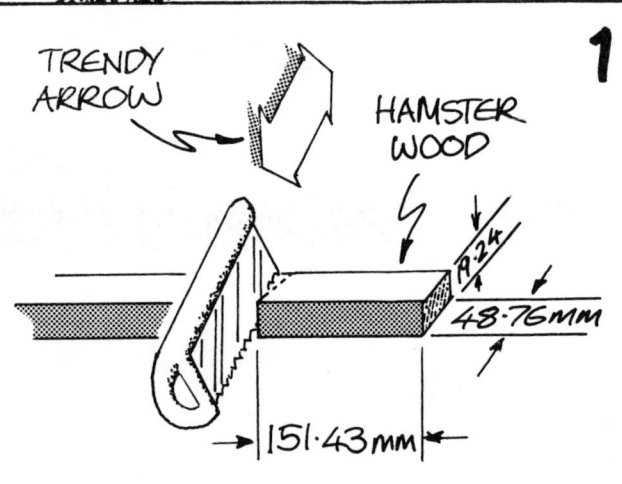

TRENDY ARROW

HAMSTER WOOD

1

R.24

48.76mm

151.43mm

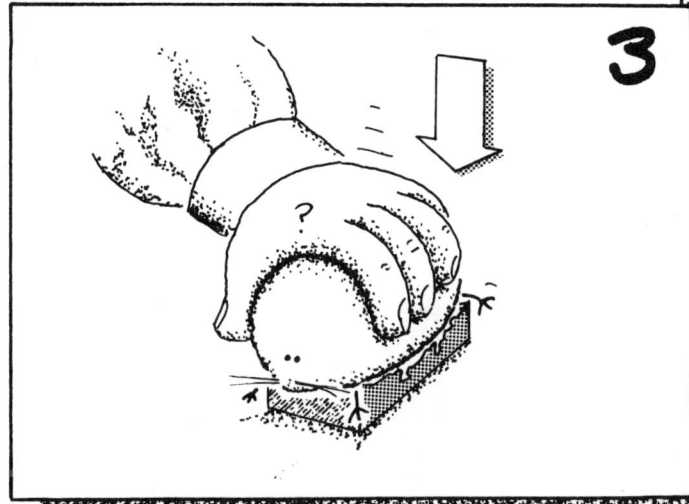

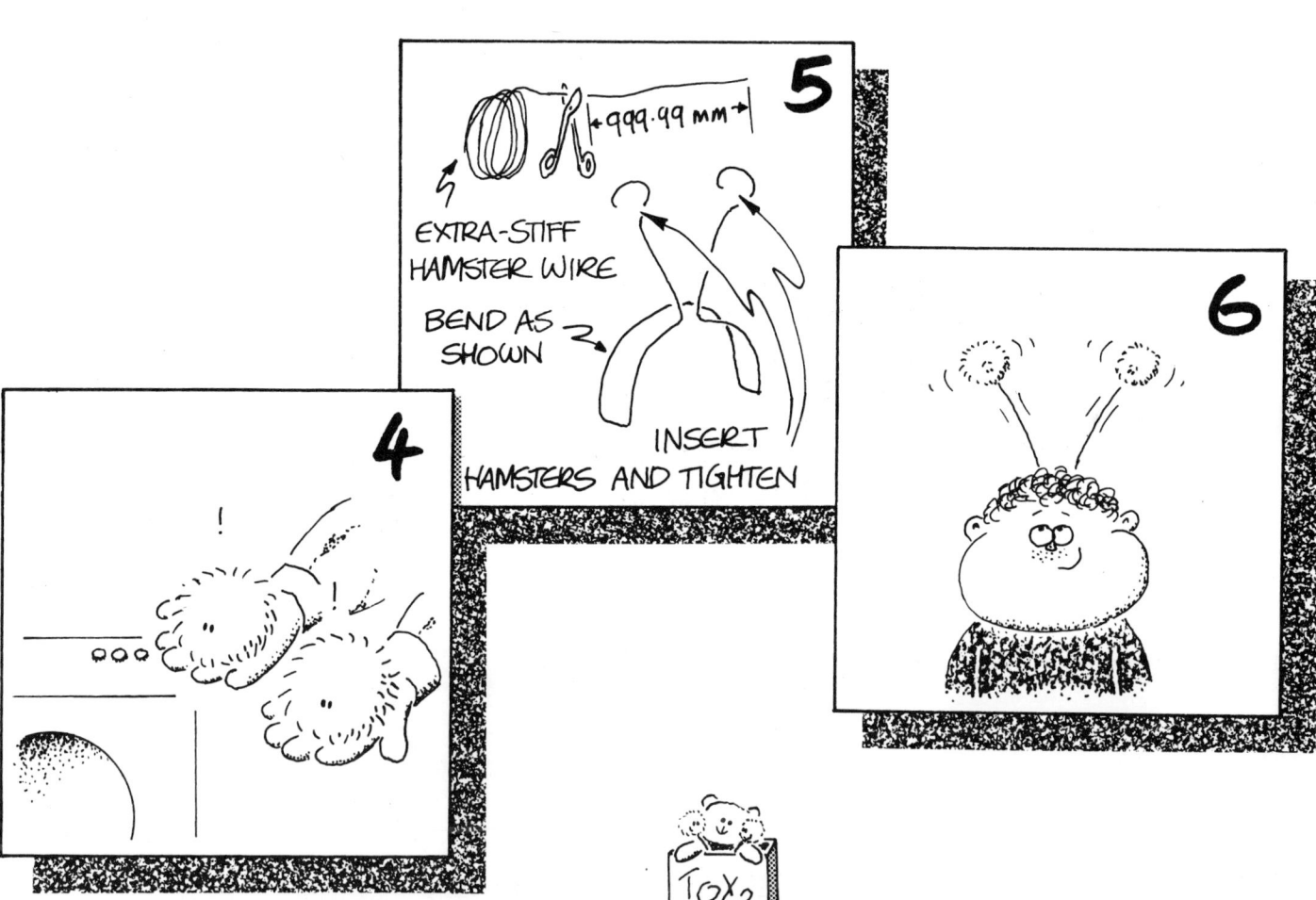

D.I.Y. HAMSTERCRAFT
FOR
THE MOTORIST

Some genuinely useful applications here. More experienced crafts-people may also like to try making an Extremely Small Car Seat Cover.

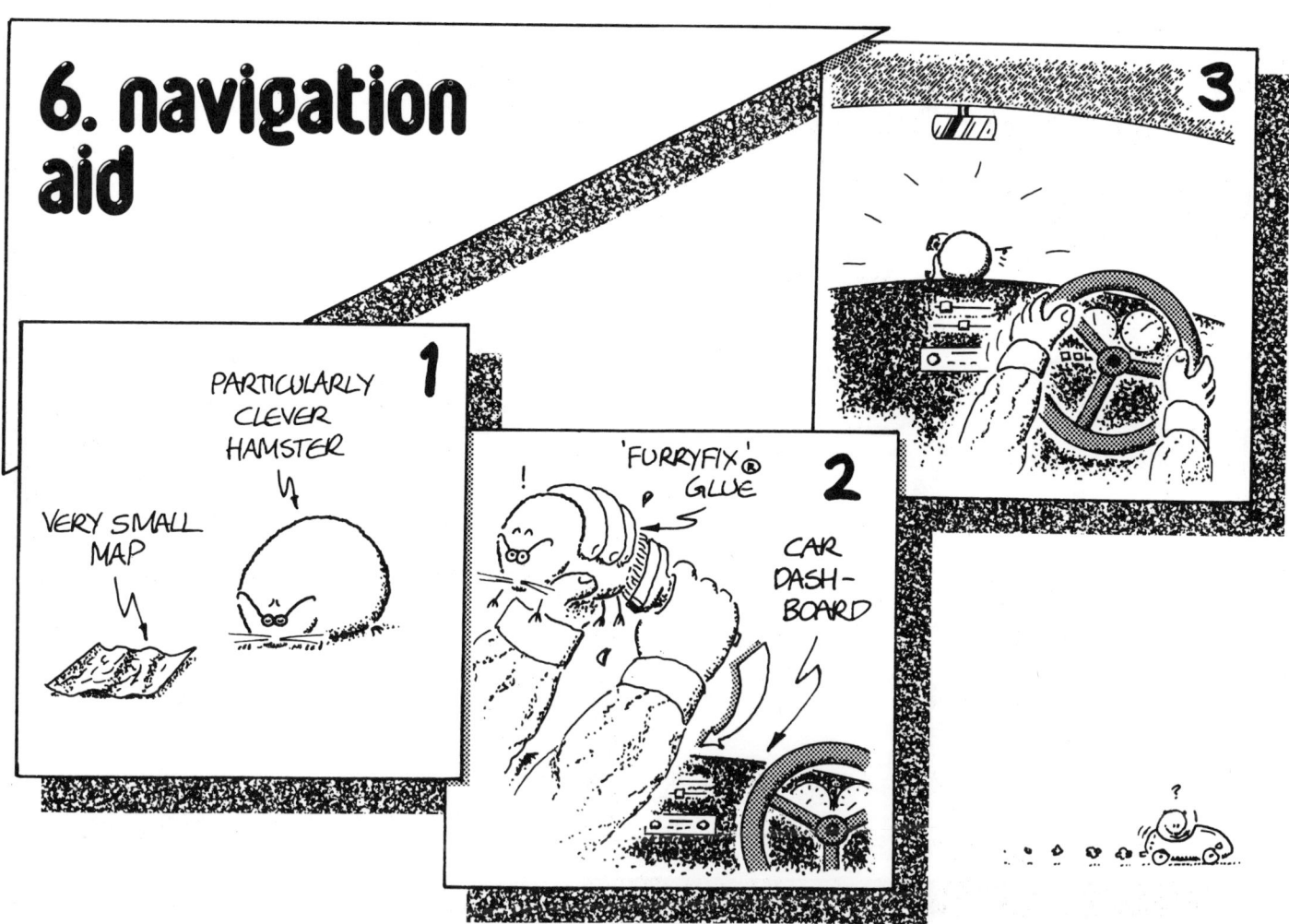

7. labour-saving car polisher

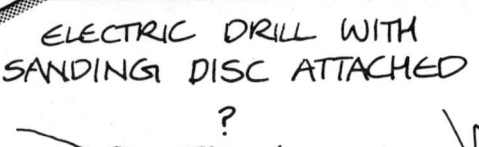

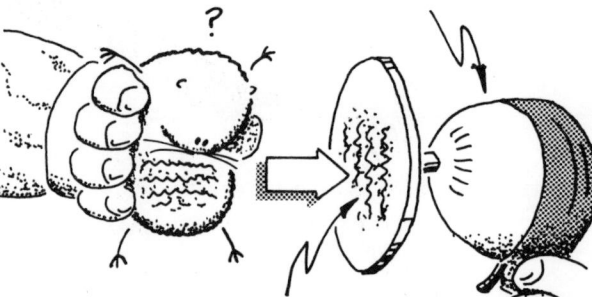

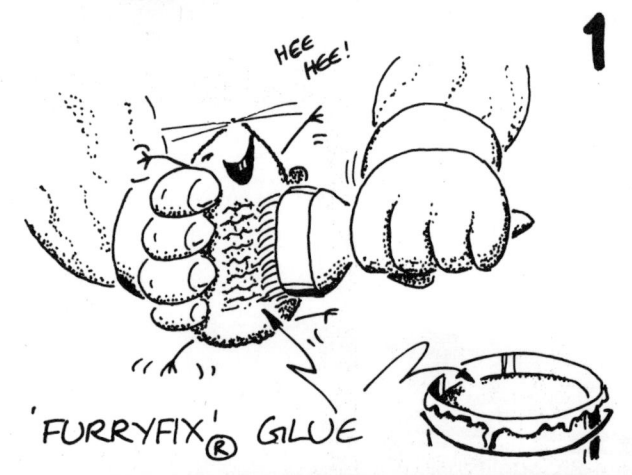

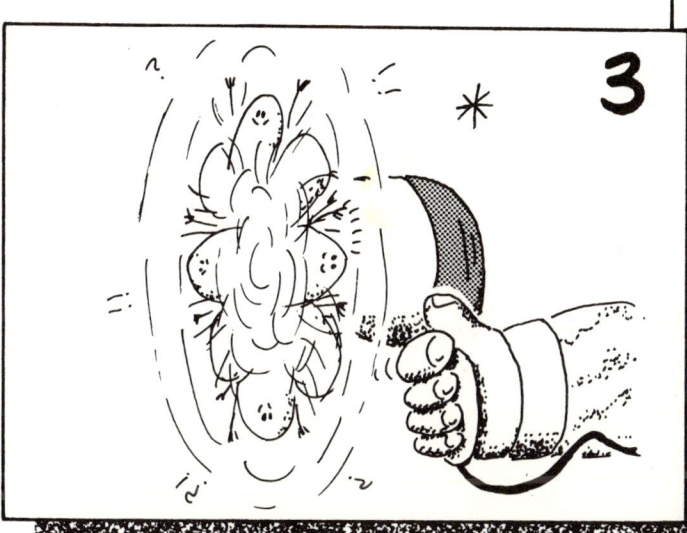

* LET GLUE DRY COMPLETELY
BEFORE TURNING ON, HAMSTER-
CRAFT LOVERS, OR YOU MAY
LOSE VALUABLE D.I.Y. TIME
FINDING THE HAMSTER

HOME DECORATION
WITH
YOUR HAMSTER

Many of the following prove how, with only a little effort, you can turn an everday hamster into an attractive ornament which you'll undoubtedly treasure until you don't.

8. novelty vase

2

PARTICULARLY
APPETISING
LOOKING
PIECE OF
LETTUCE

1

HUNGRY HAMSTER

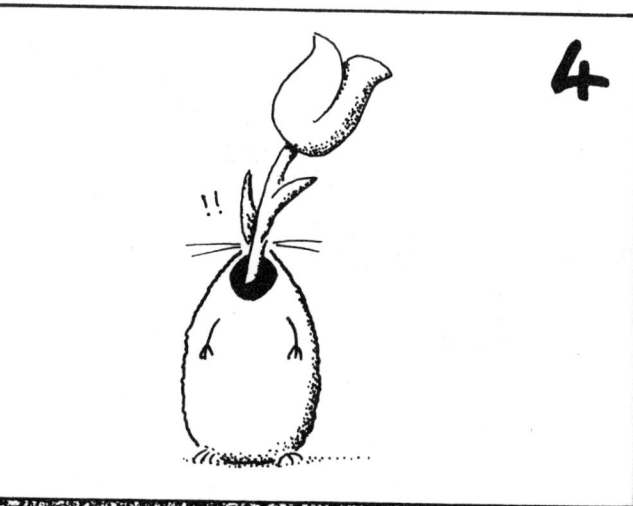

9. paperweight

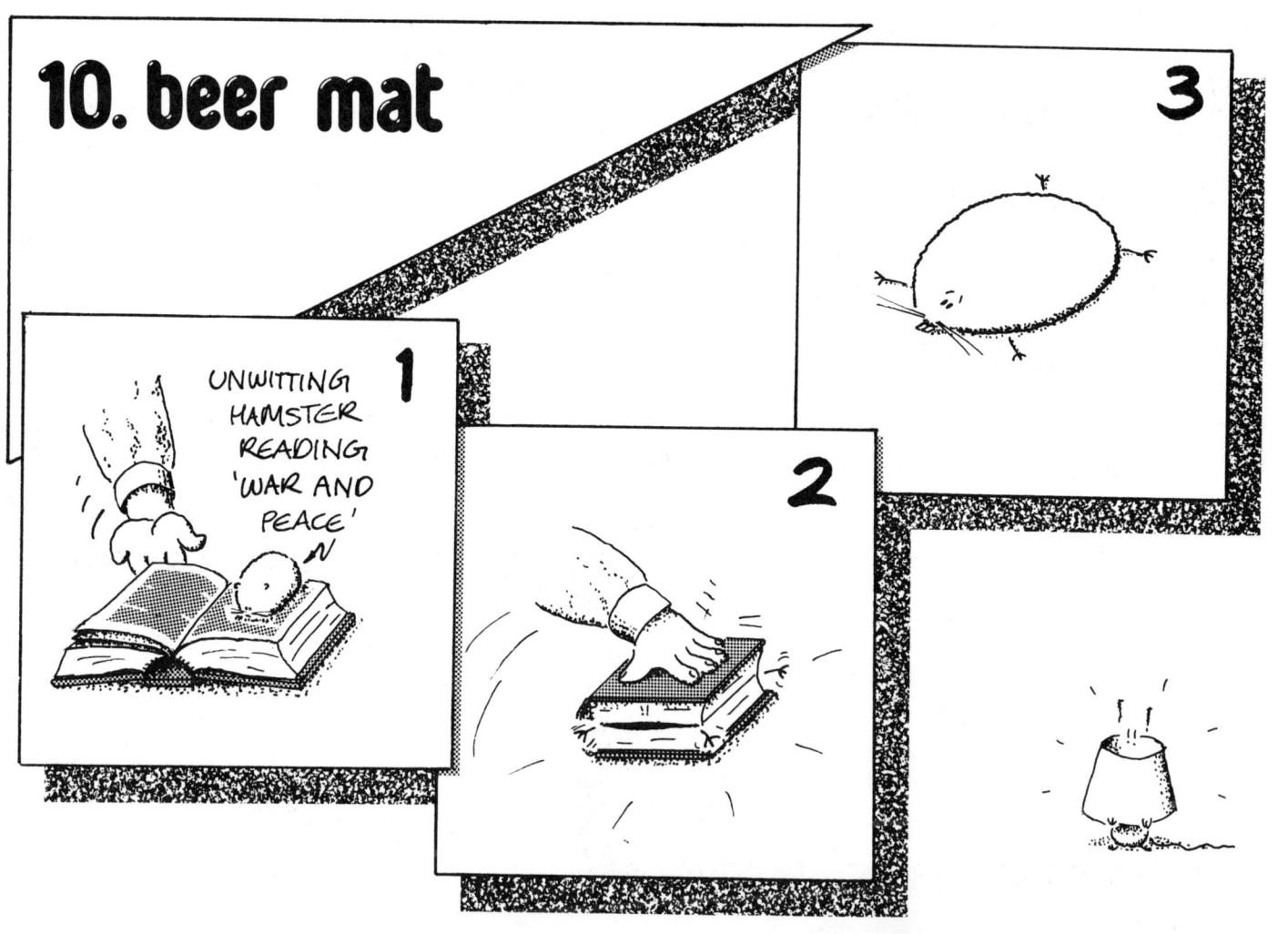

11. designer wallpaper maker

1 COOL, FUNKY HAMSTER

S*NY WALKHAMSTER

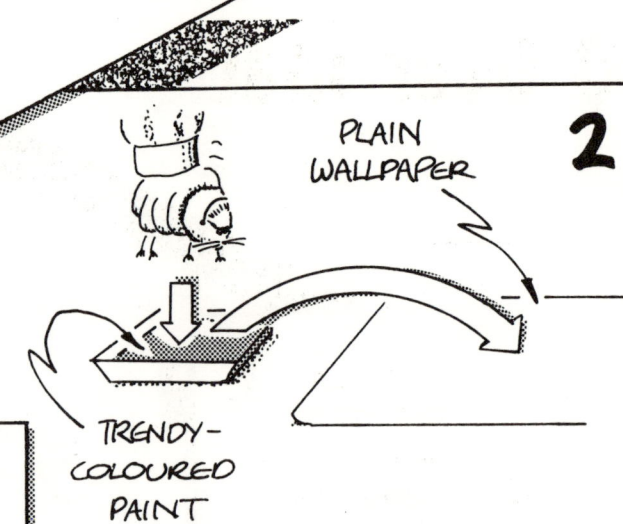

2 PLAIN WALLPAPER

TRENDY-COLOURED PAINT

INSERT COMPLETELY GROOVY
TAPE INTO WALKHAMSTER AND
TURN VOLUME RIGHT UP:
HAMSTER WILL LAPSE INTO
UNCONTROLLABLE CRAZY JIVE:

3

4

D.I.Y. HAMSTERCRAFT
FOR
THE HOUSEWIFE

Imagine the look on the face of the door-to-door brush salesman when you open the door clutching a stylish little shoebrush that you made yourself, out of a disused hamster, for only TWENTY-SEVEN PENCE! Well here's how to do it.

Particularly busy housewives may be interested to hear of a new American concept, rumoured to be on it's way over here, called 'Do-It-Themselves Hamstercraft': A method of teaching a hamster to make itself into a Very Useful Thing while you do the shopping.

12. egg cosy

TWO 4·964378 CM LONG PIECES OF HAMSTER-STRING

2

MARZIPAN HATSTAND (FOOLED YOU AGAIN)

1

UPSIDE-DOWN HAMSTER (IF YOU CAN'T GET ONE OF THESE, PUT A NORMAL ONE ON IT'S BACK)

3

TIE LEGS UP IN PAIRS AS SHOWN

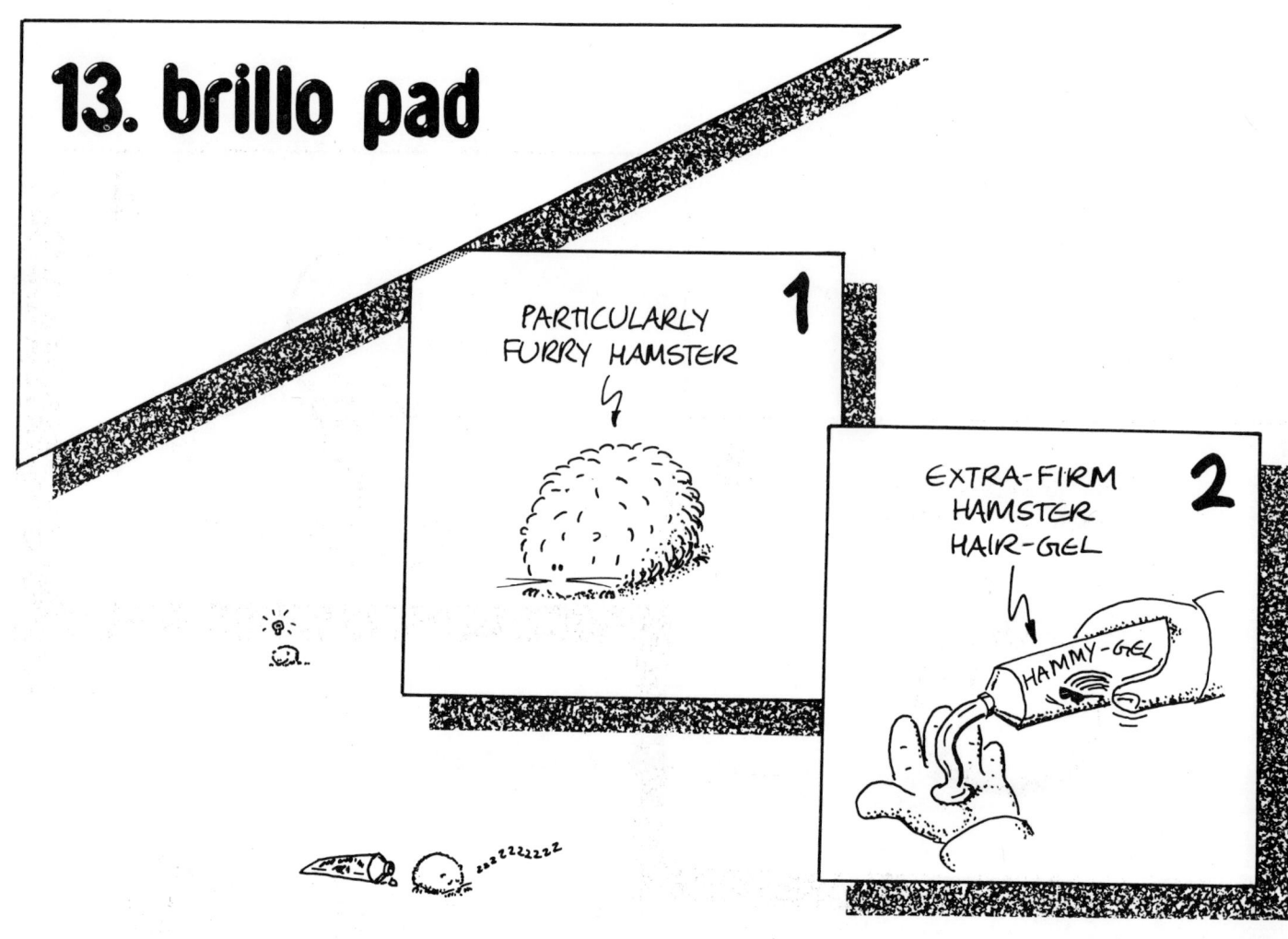

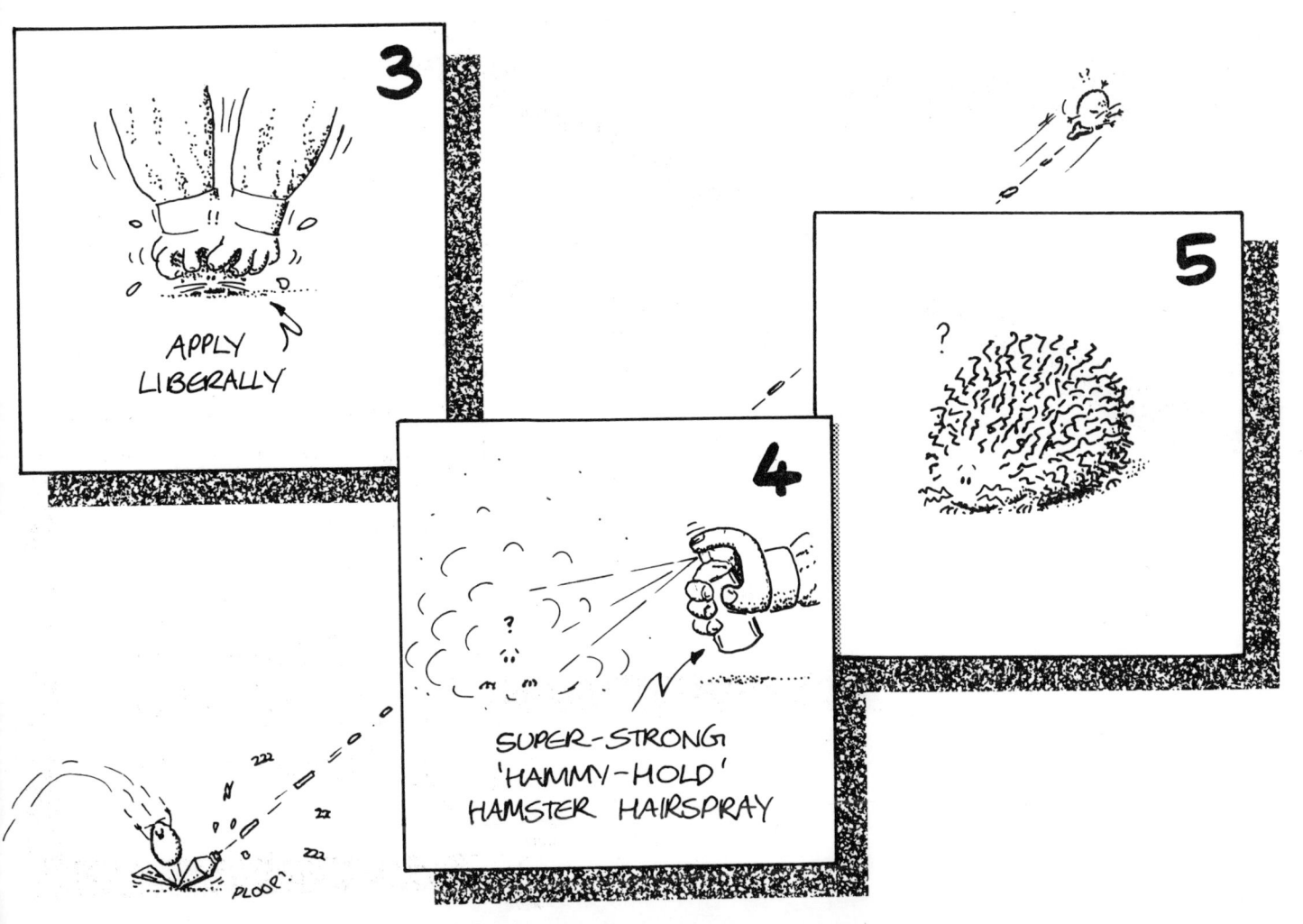

15. mug tree

2

TELL HAMSTER ONE OF MY EXTREMELY FUNNY JOKES*

1

BRIGHT RED/ PINE EGG-CUP

BRIGHT RED/ PINE HAMSTER

* 'EXTREMELY FUNNY JOKES TO TELL HAMSTERS'
— FANTASY PRESS

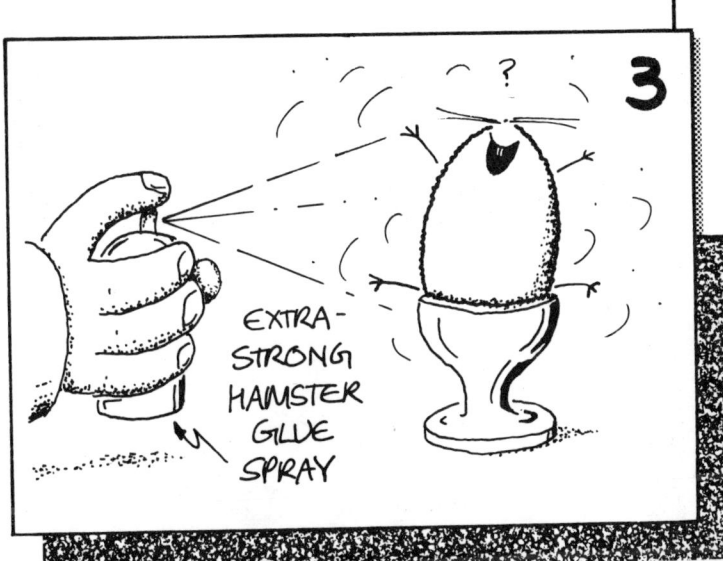

16. shoe brush

4

* SIGH *

NOTE: YOU COULD SAVE SOME D.I.Y. TIME IN THIS CASE BY SIMPLY ACQUIRING A PUNK HAMSTER. OR A SHOE BRUSH

3

HAMSTER HAIRBRUSH

SUPER-STRONG 'HAMMY-HOLD' HAIRSPRAY

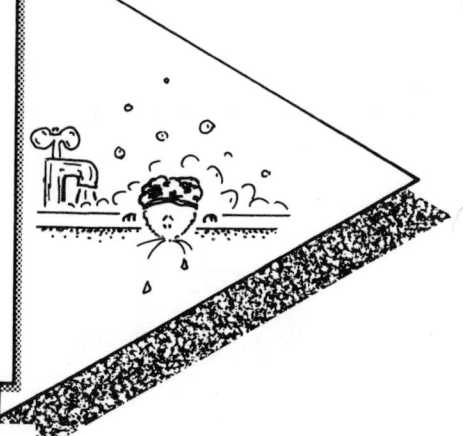

D.I.Y. HAMSTERCRAFT
IN
THE BATHROOM

Turn over the page then.

17. toilet brush

'FURRYFIX AQUASTAR'®
WATERPROOF HAMSTER
GLUE

2

1

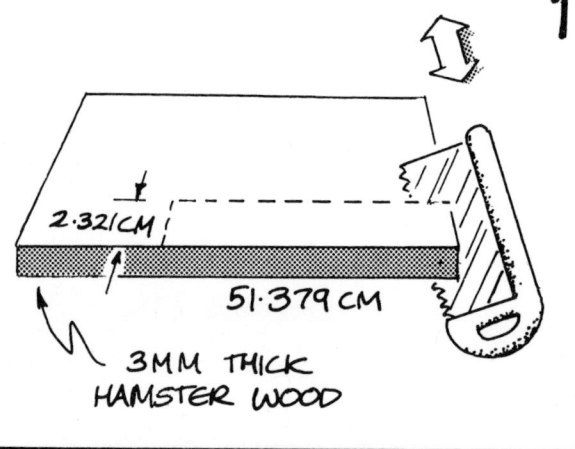

2·321 CM

51·379 CM

3MM THICK
HAMSTER WOOD

4

AQUA-LUNG*

SNORKEL*

3

* SEE 'D.I.Y. ACTION-HAMSTER-
ACCESSORY-CRAFT'
(RED HERRING PRESS) P. 36

19. toothbrush holder

1

HAMSTER READING ITS NEWSPAPER

2

EXTRA-STRONG HAMSTER GLUE SPRAY

WHEN GLUE IS DRY, CAREFULLY EXTRACT NEWSPAPER

3

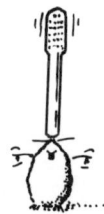

WEARING YOUR HAMSTER

A surprisingly large number of applications here: I've given instructions for three, but again more experienced craftspeople may like to try making a Wrist-Band, Winter Nose-Warmer, Sporron or Natural Look Toupé.

20. ear muffs

21. mortar-board

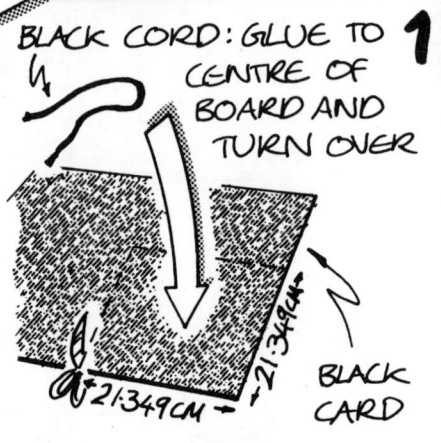

BLACK CORD: GLUE TO **1** CENTRE OF BOARD AND TURN OVER

← 21·349CM →

21·349CM

BLACK CARD

MATT BLACK HAMSTER PAINT **2**

SPLURT!

BARELY DISCERNIBLE HAMSTER

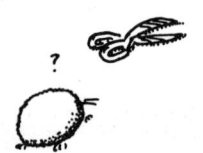

?

22. furry bow-tie

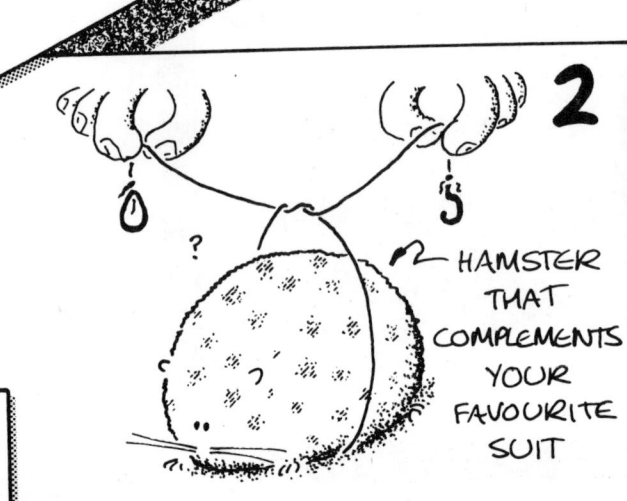

2

HAMSTER
THAT
COMPLEMENTS
YOUR
FAVOURITE
SUIT

1

38·38471627 CM LONG
PIECE OF HAMSTER
ELASTIC

TIE ON HOOK AND
EYE AS SHOWN

PULL VERY TIGHTLY AND KNOT,
THEN CLIP ROUND NECK

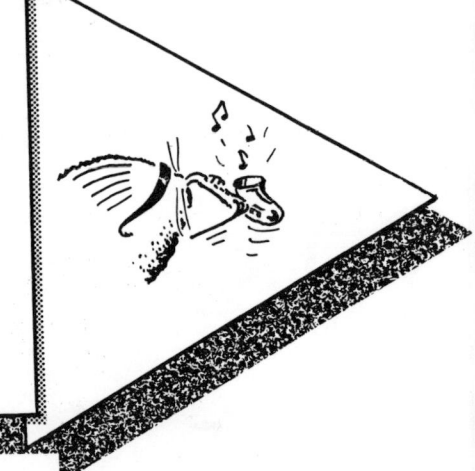

Musicians have long found hamsters useful in cleaning applications (I've given two here), but I've also heard of hamsters being used successfully as cymbal mufflers and trumpet mutes, as well as for drum damping.

Furthermore, some of you may find inspiration in the fact that I once saw a particularly attractive little harmonica case made by thoughtful joining of two hamsters.

23. euphonium cleaner

3

EXTRACT MOUTHPIECE AND INSERT HAMSTER **1**

RE-ATTACH MOUTH-PIECE AND HENCE INSERT MONOCYCLE PUMP AS SHOWN **2**

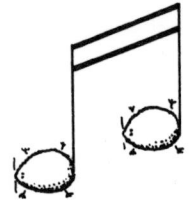

24. microphone shield

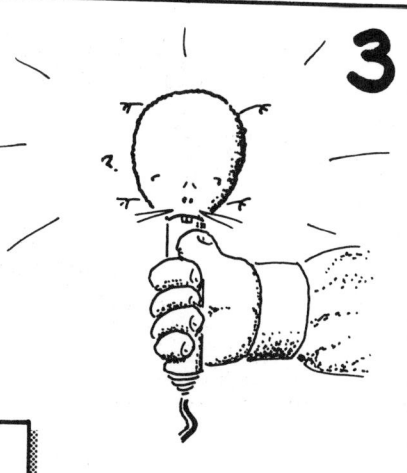

3

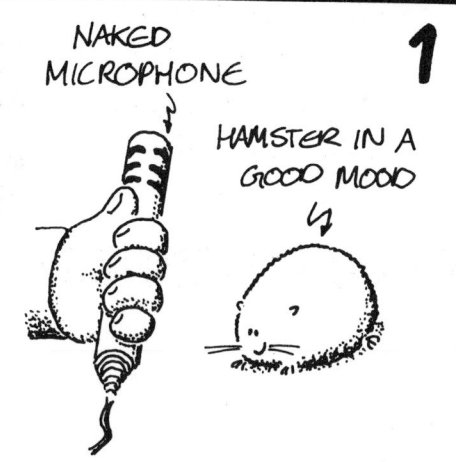

NAKED MICROPHONE

1

HAMSTER IN A GOOD MOOD

TELL HAMSTER ANOTHER ONE OF MY EXTREMELY FUNNY JOKES, AND HENCE INSERT MICROPHONE AS SHOWN

2

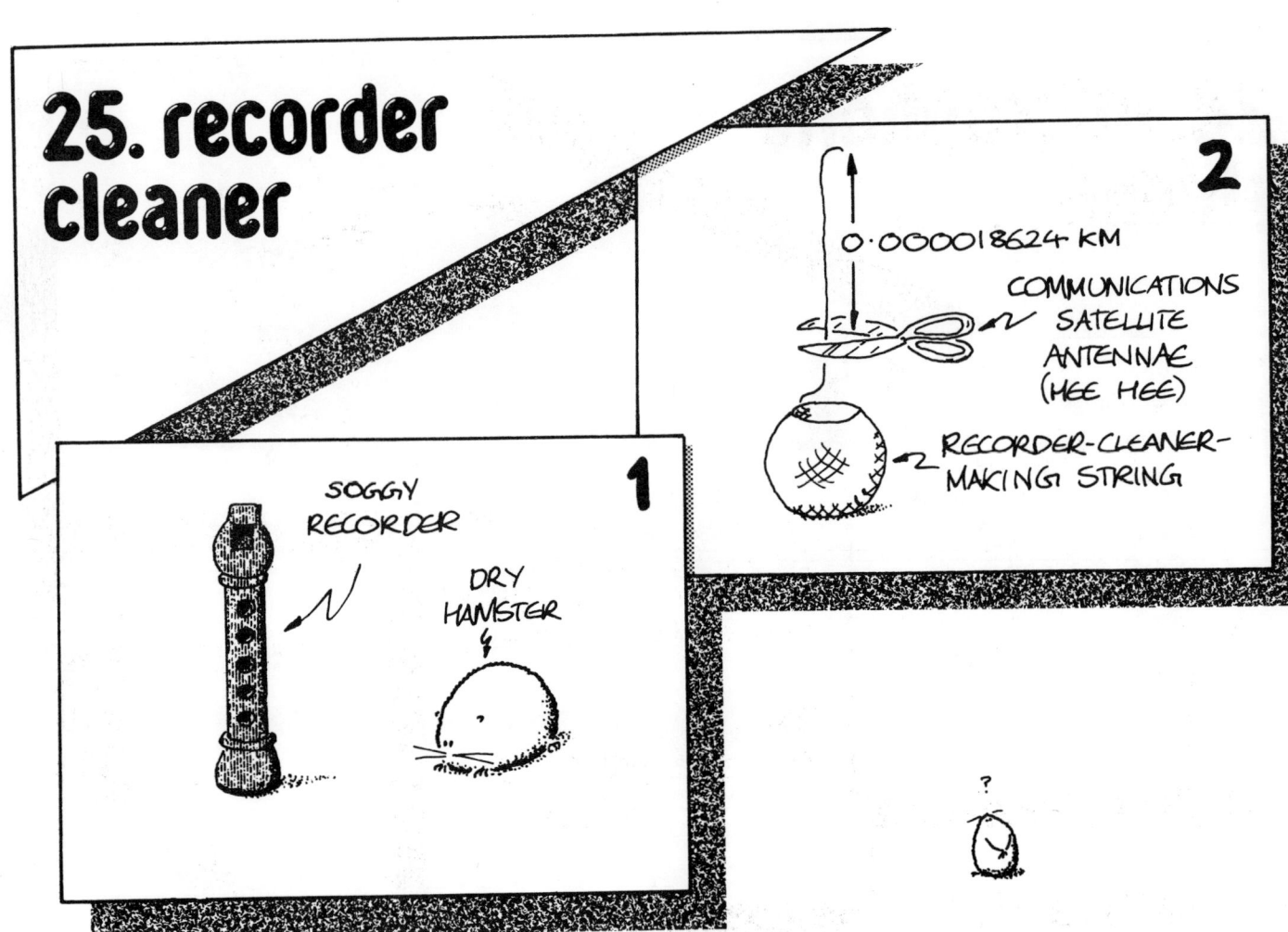

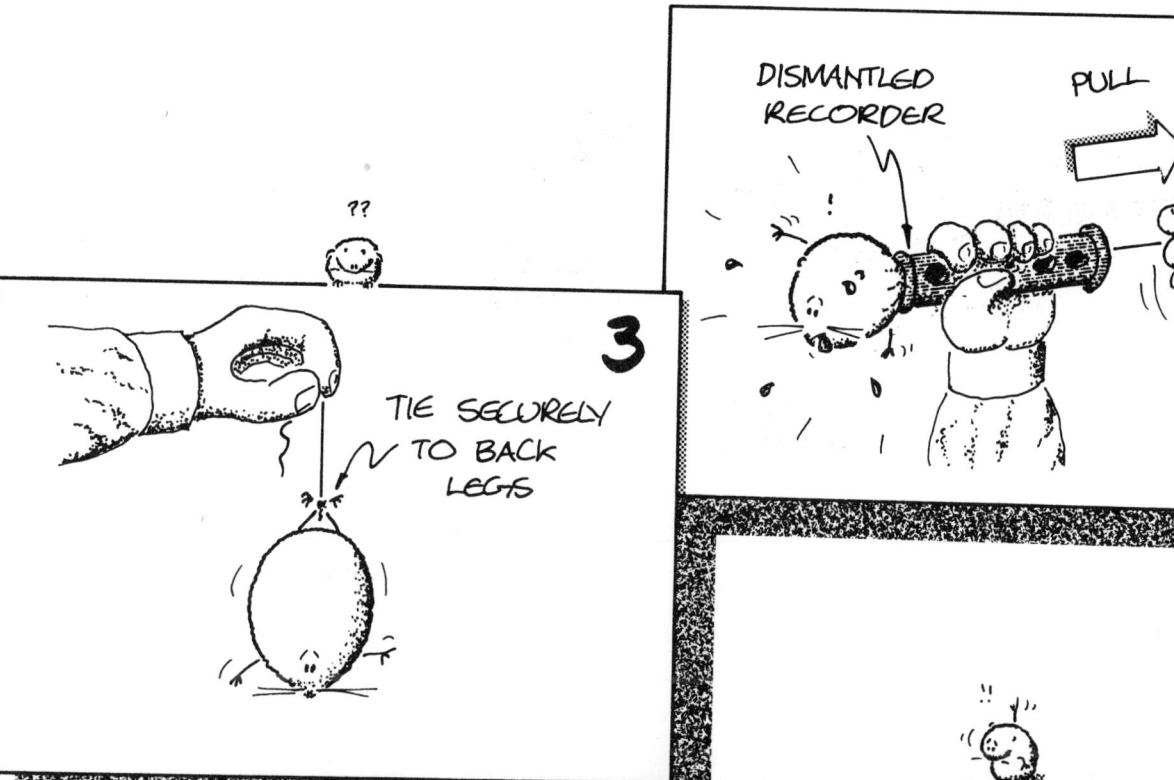